THE AMERICAN POETRY REVIEW/
HONICKMAN FIRST BOOK PRIZE

The Honickman Foundation is dedicated to the support of projects that promote spiritual growth and creativity, education and social change. At the heart of the mission of the Honickman Foundation is the belief that creativity enriches contemporary society because the arts are powerful tools for enlightenment, equity and empowerment, and must be encouraged to effect social change as well as personal growth. A current focus is on the particular power of photography and poetry to reflect and interpret reality, and, hence, to illuminate all that is true.

The annual American Poetry Review/Honickman First Book Prize offers publication of a book of poems, a $3,000 award, and distribution by Copper Canyon Press through Consortium. Each year a distinguished poet is chosen to judge the prize and write an introduction to the winning book. The purpose of the prize is to encourage excellence in poetry, and to provide a wide readership for a deserving first book of poems. *A Larger Country* is the fifteenth book in the series.

D1418251

WINNERS OF THE AMERICAN POETRY REVIEW/
HONICKMAN FIRST BOOK PRIZE

A LARGER COUNTRY

A Larger Country

Tomás Q. Morín

WINNER OF THE APR/HONICKMAN
FIRST BOOK PRIZE

The American Poetry Review
Philadelphia

Cover art: Walton Ford, *Bitter Gulfs*, 2004, watercolor, gouache, ink and pencil on paper, 60 × 119 inches (152.4 × 302.3 cm). Photo: Adam Reich. Courtesy the artist and Paul Kasmin Gallery.

Book design and composition: Valerie Brewster, Scribe Typography

Distribution by Copper Canyon Press/Consortium.

Library of Congress Control Number:
ISBN 978-0-9833008-9-2 (cloth, alk. paper)
ISBN 978-0-9663395-9-8 (pbk., alk. paper)

for D'Andra

CONTENTS

4

INTRODUCTION

Though I feel lucky to be the one to introduce Tomás Q. Morín's *A Larger Country* to what I'm sure will be a rapidly expanding readership, his poems need no one to argue for them: compulsively readable, they're as infectious and spooky and darkly humorous as the Brothers Grimm, as shapely and colloquial and eloquent as John Donne, and as skeptical and addicted to history-as-fable as Zbigniew Herbert.

Like Herbert, these poems flirt with the absurd, but underneath the deliberate oddity of some of their speakers— a troop of dancing bears, superannuated bloodhounds, name- less villagers who would seem to be living in the shadow of the concentration camp and the Gulag—their voices (again like Herbert's) are pitched more like alter egos than personae. It's as if the poet, in trying to find a way to write that is both representative and personal, took these lines of Auden's to heart. Wary of being "the darling of his grief," the poet chooses instead to join "a gang of rowdy stories where / His gift for magic quickly made him chief / Of all these boyish powers in the air..."

This gift for verbal magic is on abundant display in these lines from "On the Lam," a not-so-fond meditation on life in Utopia.

> I am on the run from this murderous peace,
> hiding in a basement from the police of Good
>   Intentions
> who want to question me about my crooked teeth,
> my ugly hands, the mohair jacket I lifted
> from someone's chair, its elbows thin, its gilded
>   buttons rotten.

The wised-up, companionable humor of one of Shakespeare's villains, both unrepentant and disdaining alibis for "screw-you" behavior, develops into this verbally brilliant, but subtle self-reckoning:

> Before I set sail for better shores
> where the children run the docks hawking
> scarves and zinnias for the jingle in your pocket,
> where their parents still know how to fight and
>   what's better
> how to lose themselves in anger, reluctant anger,
> the kind we were granted long ago on the eighth day
> when He was no longer busy hiding justice in the fang
> of each beast, remorse in the shaft of each claw,
> and all that lives in my teeth is regret,
>   sweet regret, pacing its network of black caves…

The way Morín's imagination ramps up to the eighth day of creation when the peaceable kingdom begins to tear itself apart, not out of justice or remorse, but out of sheer blood-lust, is both comic and chilling and gleefully refreshing in its directness about human motives. But the passage deepens even more in the last two lines, when the speaker's teeth become a network of black caves, cavities of regret—but a regret that the speaker savors, as if our desire for universal harmony was inextricable from a darker desire to court our own pain.

This central dilemma announces in *A Larger Country* a poet who has something to say, and who has found the odd and exact and new way of saying it, so that you can feel what is new and odd and exact in what and how he's saying it.

This sensation of uniqueness is how Eliot once character-
ized "genuine poetry." In Morín's poem "A Dress Rehearsal
for the Apocalypse," he writes of the exhumation of Miklós
Radnóti from a mass grave, a Hungarian, Jewish poet who
died on a death-march. What could have been an exercise
in what Derek Walcott once called "the stock elegiac," turns
into something much more troubling, and serves as an excel-
lent example of what Eliot meant by "genuine." Whereas
"On the Lam" demanded a certain extravagance of speech,
the language here achieves its uniqueness through restraint
and understatement:

> …he rose from the darkest beds in Abda
> after six years, dirty-eared and unshaven,
> and brought a message we could not abide
> because he was still a man in a man's shape.

But I don't want to give you the idea that Morín is
relentlessly grim. Even in this passage, the risen poet seems
to flaunt his dirty ears and unshaven mien. Despite the dis-
enchanted recognition of the last line, the poet still manages
to project a certain gaiety, even an insouciant defiance, of
the horrors of history. Or consider these lines from "Blood-
hounds," as deadpan as they are whimsical, in which the
bloodhounds "do what celebrities do when they fall / from
favor, they answered the call of Hollywood" to appear on the
set of a new show called "Singing School:"

> …They were a hit
> because karaoke was fashionable again,
> as was suffering, as was pity,

and so the episodes kept coming, cabled
week after week into the dark living rooms
where our beautiful, intelligent race sat
in the raw hours, attentive, sniffing the air,
waiting for a sign in those throaty baritones
that we might yet find another life.

Sometimes, as in that last line, you have to say it simply. And yet this final declaration, with its skeptical emphasis on "yet," makes clear the deeper, and deeply complex links among suffering, pity, and yes, karaoke — that act of Hollywoodish impersonation in which we lip-synch our way, through someone else's troubles or joys, into our own joys and sorrows and shadowy desires. Not so different, after all, than what Morín does in making himself known through his personae to his potential readers.

As to those readers, I'd say that a poet like Tomás Q. Morín, who has taken the measure of karaoke, as well as the dirt dug from a mass grave, is a poet here to stay. His poems have already enlarged our conception of the country of writing and feeling, and I trust that we can look forward to a long and generous future in which he continues to explore how "we might yet find another life."

Tom Sleigh

A LARGER COUNTRY

I

LAIKA

In '57 Sputnik 2 carried her into space
where the first bark went unheard.
Did she lick herself or nip at the whir
of the fan in that cabin? These concerns
were not important to science, unlike velocity,
heart rate, time of death. When my faith
in justice wavers, I embrace my inner Greek
and butcher the sky, carve out a swath of stars
catching a curve of light millions of years old
and pretend it's the outline of a dog,
half-husky, half-terrier. I retreat to this fantasia
when another report of animal cruelty
soils further the already filthy news.
It was years before we knew
she didn't last more than five hours
in that wretched kennel, weightless,
and think of the trash she could have rooted,
the black boots she could have shined
with a few well-placed curtsies
in deference to the great mutts of history—
think Khrushchev and Kennedy.
Sweet Laika, it has been decades since my last confession,
and my sins are many: in Kathmandu I herded strays
through the alleys, ticked their foreheads
and paws red, wept in gratitude when they licked my face
because now they might let me pass
through the gates of heaven with only a tender snarl
for having diced garlic, may the bulbs forgive me,
in the kitchens of Laos. I went my whole life
without seeing a dog struck by a car and then it was there—

have mercy upon the pronoun, I didn't get out—
in the mirror, watching the Chevys and Fords,
pounding the pavement with its tail before the truck
hauling from Georgia who knows what,
and it was in that other Georgia, the colder one,
where I entered the life of a minor scientist,
hunting the bakeries of Moscow for tea cake
one day, the trash heaps the next for any dog
the size of a breadbox, one not much bigger
than the tabby at the foot of my bed dreaming
about the injustice of wings, unaware of my past
allegiances, that I was born under the sign of the dog,
that I have lived and died a traitor to my own kind.

THE FAMILY ARTIST

Schneiderpüppe. He had carried the weight
of this word on his tongue for weeks,
not able to remember what it meant
until he stared through a dirty window
at a member of that ancient race.

Struck by something like pity, he gave
the tiny woman behind the counter
whose name he couldn't pronounce
the few dollars she was asking
and carried the tailor's doll home, wedged

under one arm, past the caged-in lawns
and up cracked stairs. She is a she,
he found out, they having made small talk
while on the bus, while he shimmied
his furniture up against the walls.

She didn't complain once,
not even when he tossed her high
over his head like a ballerina,
one rough hand on each hip
or when the bulb popped unexpectedly

and they had to sit in the dark.
All night they traded stories
about lost loves, last loves,
and it was difficult for them
to know how much to hold back

when it was impossible to see
each other's expressions,
to read *that was enough*
mapped desperately
on the other's eyes. So they continued

until dawn and even stomped a salsa
when a neighbor squawked
his stereo too loud. At first light,
he stood, thought, then framed her
with the square of his hands

and recognized the silhouette
of his grandmother, the thick waist
and the narrow shoulders.
Not wanting to be cruel, he begged
her forgiveness first then sanded

her breasts into a cloud of cream
flurries until each was flat
and smooth as the floor
they had eaten breakfast on.
He brushed away the shavings

and pressed his ear hard
against her now warm chest and listened
to the thunks of snowbound cars
starting and stopping outside.
Since she was hollow, he poured

bags of white tinsel through the hole
at her neck. In his eagerness
he hadn't noticed all his effort
escaping out the bottom
until he saw the young neighbors

in the window across the street
staring as if they had never seen
a *schneiderpüppe* with loose bowels
dust a floor with snow. The hole patched,
he poured at her neck again and mixed

in cut apricots this time, dried, pungent,
so she could come to life in the nose
as well as the eye
because that is how she had lived
and how could he ever forget the smell

of the last time he sat by her bed,
the one with the rubber wheels,
or the promise she had forced him to make
in a language he could no longer speak,
to live like a brute mark that she was here.

CASTRATO

Seaside. It had all started well enough
for the last child in a family of five
when he arrived in his mother's fifty-first year.
Omens had announced his coming
to the small village for days. The fish
had seemed to multiply within everyone's nets
and at first, all the signs were of plenty.
This good fortune continued until the sun
was driven away and the winds off the water
bowed the trees so that they looked
like penitents kissing the ground.
After the storm the light crept back
and everyone saw how the waves had beaten
the thin face of their beach jagged.

Ten years later, the boy child, a gifted singer,
has his parents take his life in their hands.
What happened in the intervening years,
you wonder? Exactly what one would expect
for a boy of the nineteenth century
in a hamlet surrounded by mountains
and endless ocean: he stole fruit
in the moonlight from the orchard
at the edge of town, played shepherd
with the neighbor girls, loved
his father and mother and sisters.

When the scar between his legs had hardened
and given up its anger, they shipped him
to a conservatory where he never grew

another inch. Bored, he trapped chaffinches
and cooked them in the papal garden,
provoked fights with the angelic boys
in the choir and broke the bones
of his face against their beautiful hands.

What do you call a gifted soprano
with no balls who is too ugly
to play the heroine, is never tall enough
for the role of the hero? Wait a quarter century
and you can fast forward past the floggings,
the endless sermons, the giggles under alders
with curious girls, busted noses, carped
sisters with chubby boys, the innumerable
nights of sleeplessness. Better to skip all this
unpleasantness and descend the last rise
toward the coast where you can stroll the docks
in the short light of winter, get lost
in the cloudbank, let the sea ripen
in your hair, scan the flat water
for the handsome young men clutching
their oars, straining to hear the tiny figure
of their uncle who is on a stool gutting a fish,
who is waiting for the sound of wood slapping
water in the distance, whose lips will bloom
and unravel a sharp tune for the sour air.

PRESIDENTIAL PORTRAIT

Upon first seeing the shadow-boxed collage
of the 43rd president, I thought,
his face is a kaleidoscope of bodies. Later that night,
I stared at my own face in the window, bent, fluid,
like a dying animal's.
In the morning, I started an ode to the artist
who cut out the women he found in magazines
like coupons in order to fashion Bush's face.
I wanted to applaud
the cheap irony, but kept returning
to the blameless curve of an arm, or the idea,
rather, of that arm, and of tapered fingers
a father would have cradled while crossing the street,
or the wet feet of someone's daughter
hopping in her galoshes
over piles and piles of yesterday's snow
now turned the color of traffic.
I couldn't escape. Even when I slept,
he was there. When I woke I told him,
"Enough already, sincerity is dead…"
but he only smiled and seemed about to stumble
into a speech on the mutilated millennium
or how nations could beautify their hinterlands
the American way, a dollar at a time.

Starved for affection, he follows me
everywhere like a puppy. At church
he tears the bread and laps the wine
because he'll believe in anything once.
Whenever we enter a grocery store

mothers will cover their children's eyes
because I was all wrong, you see, about the fingers
and the arms and the feet, even the blame,
most of all the blame,
because the portrait I saw was a fog, a bank of pixels
teased to within a blot of themselves
so that I couldn't see the array of vulvas,
each carefully trimmed anus
jig-sawed into a patch of pubic hair
to make the sweep of his coy lips which are now
in the shower with me crooning "Love Me Daddy Blues"
in his best Bessie Smith. After I've toweled
and shaved, slipped into my best suit à la Keats,
I'll sit at my desk
cloaked in a fabric so prehistoric
it'll be hard to tell what is more monstrous,
the proud head wobbling on the couch
or the parti-colored clown lost over a blank page
for what seems like years, searching
its deep white for a pattern, a single sentence
to drape over the monsters of the world.

BRITISH BIRDS IN MANHATTAN

The horses crossing the cobblestone
    startle the starlings
and as I lift my arms to calm them

    it might as well be 1890
and I might as well be Eugene Schieffelin
    ambling in Central Park

with cages under my arms, my pockets
    full of seed, muttering
my *Henry IV*. When the flock returns

    it's for a sandwich,
half-eaten, tossed by a woman
    with bird hips

whistling "Expressway to Your Heart,"
    who'll never know
she just nailed her part in a story

    about good intentions,
nor that it will end somewhere in the city
    on a street sign

when rush hour meets the stony,
    sausage-scented
breath of starlings calling out

    in a perfectly pitched
American key *shit fuck bastard*.
    Most people smile,

some even wince, but one dreamer
    will always blink
heavily and want to leave his car to hunt

    the park's muck
for Hitchcock's lonely love birds
    but he won't

because it's not 1890 and he knows
    there are no more
claims to stake for art. Having heard

    this song before,
he'll continue the anonymous crawl
    toward home

where he stars in all the old dramas
    as Beauty
with huge, haunted hands,

    a Roman nose
built for love, and a wrecked,
    sentimental heart

that sighs like a bug in the beak.

WHILE WAITING FOR THE RESURRECTION

To find my home in one sentence, concise,
as if hammered in metal.
— CZESŁAW MIŁOSZ

My dear Czesław, it was only just yesterday
I discovered you sleeping in the garden
behind our building. I had long since given up

on raising anything to maturity until I found you
held close by last season's tomatoes, your quiet face
already overrun with summer's weeds,

your thinned hair an industrious highway
of night's creatures. I know what you really wanted
was a sturdy sentence that would move meaning

patiently along the slick backs of verbs and nouns.
Nevertheless, consider how your bones will strengthen
after the shallow culverts fill and empty their beds;

imagine how much richer the soil will be
upon drinking the blood of your blood or how fat
the squash will grow feeding between your legs

or how good they will taste fried with slivers of lemon.
This year, I expect we will have much to harvest
because I know the carrots and peas will love you

for your good Polish clay and the zucchini will sleep
well against your hard belly. I know the countryside
suits you better, so I ask you to forgive my city yard

for its smallness and the buildings above your head
for their constant roar of toilets and I ask you
to forgive the rain that never reaches the earth

and the daily rituals of cats and dogs; forgive me
for the indignant way I will deny you
to my neighbors and for the silences I will keep

when I sit down with my children to taste
the salty soup you helped me make tonight
with the wild onions I pulled from your feet.

THE HOME FRONT

The war was supposed to have been swift
but then the seasons changed, and then the years
came and went. What remained the same were the faces,
long and dark, of the wives perched in the windows,
the lean sisters walking the streets in summer
interrogating me with their eyes: Why
are you here and not there? I didn't have an answer,
so I followed them home and filled the empty chairs
for a while, wore the clothes of their husbands
and brothers, told stories about my bad back.

Every morning the neighbors would tell me
how I had been missed up the street, around the block,
that someone's mother had wept alone
over her soup while music blared upstairs,
how a widow had fallen asleep, her ear to the rug,
listening for the swallows trapped in the floor.

I could hardly bear these tales of suffering
so I did what anyone else would have done
and rose at dawn to fight the jay and the rat
for the right to scour the doorsteps
and the alley-ways for yesterday's papers.

In my sink I worked the death-heavy
tabloids with soap, dashes of phlegm,
until I had a paste I could fashion a forehead
or an ear out of, all the geography of a face
like my own. When the landlord asked
what was with the leaning towers of newspapers,

the cans of flesh-tone paint, the pile of hair
growing in the corner, I told him
I needed reinforcements, to which he shrugged
and simply said, "Don't burn the place down."

By month's end I was on every couch,
shirt starched, cologned, wearing my best slacks,
watching the dining tables bear the weight
of the empty plates, the solemn cutlery,
while on the outskirts of some distant city
ringed in fire, someone's son sat in a hole dreaming
of the black phone on the bureau.

During the day I keep the dogs company,
the parakeets that whistle Vivaldi,
watch the place while everyone works,
my silhouette in the window a warning
to would-be thieves. As the weeks turn
into months, I settle in and learn family trees
by heart and leave my hair on the pillow.
Before long the honeymoon is over
and I am swimming in wine, am forgetting
to fix the faucet, to walk the trash to the curb,
to buy flowers on anniversaries,
and so they yell and scold while I sit and stare
at the meatloaf, contemplate the beets,
their shapely roots, all that vertiginous color
which makes me swoon and want to swap apologies,
to welcome the return of another season of peace.

OUR PROPHETS

It shouldn't have surprised me while reading
Gorky's remembrance of Tolstoy and devouring chicken
on a blanket in view of the muddy waters
that I should see a parakeet misnamed the Quaker parrot
by some scientist poet with a sense of humor,
not to mention fashion, because he found modesty
in the way their lime color drapes over
their backs and down each wing in a way that
reminds one of a key lime pie; though not
the one with the dome of meringue which resembles
the dress of a house finch, rather the wobbly
body of the sad supermarket doppelganger;
the impostor with the God-awful filling
tinted green by they of the white aprons
and soufflé hats who no doubt assume we are all children
of Truth and would thus not know how to suffer
a yellow-white pie with lime in its name;
much less something important like the rapture
that came and went last week
for which the stores baked a special angel food cake
labeled *Manna* and stuffed with so many
mulberries it bled through; and no one I know vanished
and perhaps it was a rapture that extinguished
the tribe of Attsurs from which the parrot came
that Tolstoy recounts to Gorky as possessing
the last traces of the history of its lost people
in its sickled tongue. And how long did it take the Attsur
scholar after he took the bird home, fed it dates
and schnitzel from his own lips, to translate
the precious words for "mama" and "wine,"

"kitty" and "bye-bye," and when the rapture comes again
tomorrow and we finally vanish as predicted,
what bird will speak for us if not our monkish
parakeet souring in the oak above us
like a cheap piece of pie
that calls out "hungry, hungry, hungry"?

2

DUMB LUCK

There are some things I should tell you
beforehand: I was born on a bed
covered quickly with a quilt. I stepped

my bare feet into the new world
of a lamp-lit room in the country.
Because of a broken driveshaft we stayed,

my mother and I, among the witch hazel
straddled houses and the buzzard-heavy
poles rising upward like wooden angels.

She had meant to rest on the bleached
linens of the Sisters of Mercy
hospital, and if only I had not come early

I might have been named Olaf
or Sven after one of the three doctors
in town. Why does any of this matter

you wonder, what is the point
of unwinding the threads of this life
I will never have? My mother wanted

a daughter so at five I dressed flowers
with my hair and answered to Margaret
as she watched my face darken

with all the coming furies of boyhood.
If they had conceived me sooner
I might now remember my father

taking his streaked hand to my back
and lifting me into the stunned air
of April, although common sense suggests

I wouldn't have remembered the moment
nor his face or the light rain tapping
its fingers on our shingled roof

like a deaf man pounding Chopin
away on the keys of an unstringed piano
because he believes what he was told,

that there is joy in our sheer movement
of a thing from A to B, that a sound
made realizes its purpose when it fills

a silence because that is what we do
when we are born. We waken and cry
to the silent walls and a radio gone hush,

to the earthbound rooster and hens
bent in the yard because we are finally
in the world we always said we wanted.

A MODEL FOR THE PRIESTHOOD

In thigh-deep water we lashed the air with our rods
and re-examined the eternal questions: tongue, eye, nose—

which one has the shortest route to the brain, the heart:
which nails would you release first if it were given to you,

the feet or the hands: if Chickamauga meant river of the dead
then what were the implications for all bodies of water?

He filled the sink with the trout who hit our lines,
crossed himself once, twice, then renamed and cut each one

—their vague eyes rolling—while I made ready to gently knuckle
each flayed beloved with garlic and thyme, an American John

to his American Jesus, humming my crazy songs
over the black faces of the pans I baptized in butter.

"The dead will only suffer butter," he liked to say,
as I dropped a shoulder and tumbled each head into a basket

for the tabby in the woods who never failed to pick up
the scent of resurrection in our mouths, who would chirp

and follow us even unto the shaky outhouses where we rocked
and returned the dead to the earth from where they came.

THE LIFE OF THE PARTY
Leaving Terezin

My brothers wait for me with cigars in their mouths,
debating the price of cabbage and the virtues of sleep,
and my sisters having just arrived, hang their shawls
in the hallway and then sit and redden their faces
over white cups of tea. The train whistles
and the sleeping boy beside me just stirs
long enough to touch his father's leg, to point
out the window at the large flocks of men
swinging their picks, spading their way
to the noiseless center of an imagined market
in Beijing where they will buy the best silk
their good looks can get and then rose their cheeks
until they look like grandmothers on holiday
in the Near East.

               Beyond the men, in the smoky
clods of dirt I can see the lost children of this land
sneaking behind the silent showers to peek
at the concrete and its people. I consider
how long their eyes wandered before they turned
and took chalk to paper, coal to wood.
How would you see the world after that,
would the night teach you anything about comfort,
would you still marvel at your red-faced mother
pulling her clay head from the mouth of an oven,
her hair overcome with the smells of new bread?
A girl drops her chalk, bends and picks up
a long feather of smoke with her nose
and then begins to pity everything from the black
throats of chimneys to the huffing trains
logging through the countryside the baked bones

of her fathers and mothers.
                    I brood and mouth
the words of a question I cannot ask, cannot
voice to the unclean air: O little ones, would you have
looked any longer or moved the chalk any slower
if you had known that one day you'd be loved again
and again by the words in a book or that I would crawl
under your sky on the morning of my birthday,
bundled tightly in the seat of my car, your drawings
in my lap and on the floor between my feet
the last pies—one apple, one cherry—my mother
made now beginning to tear their metal faces?

WINTER

There is a church with a steeple and houses whose roofs
mirror the slope of the church's roof which is
meant to dominate the center of the canvas;
such was the nature of faith in the sixteenth century.
If you lose interest in the architecture the snow
will always yoke you back in, as will the barren trees
that make your eyes dart from one to the other
in search of a nest, a bird, a remnant of a bird even,
and when you fail to accomplish even this small task
you will turn to the ice and the skaters because there is
nothing else to turn to and because there is certainty
in their movements, and this comforts you, the slicing
of smooth spirals and the hand-holding and the red noses—
only there are no skaters as you had once thought and now
you are confused and all you can see are the people being beaten
with clubs and branches from the trees you had worried over,
and then you notice the empty lake in the background,
the greater body of water in the frame,
and you tell yourself the ice will crack, the snow melt,
and this is something which makes you feel better
because it is a scene you have witnessed before.

EGG MINISTRY

In a grim henhouse I find the faithful
clucking about the rapture,
and whether heaven is truly shallow and fresh
like a box of straw waiting for birth.
All eggs will break, I assure them, the laws of gravity
and rise from china bowl and carton alike,
from the unswept thresholds of batteries,
up past fire escape and silo, cloud and bird.
As they consider this, a reddish, bouquet-crested hen
nods to sleep and glides to jumbled scenes
of desert sand and sticky, Egyptian hands
grinding a bold, yolk-yellow powder
for mixing with egg and water—
to paint skin, no doubt. Later, Giotto
will use it to ignite his poor saints' heads,
while Botticelli will mute it for his Madonnas
whose petite, exhausted faces
in the flight-heavy dreams of hens would surely flake
and having flaked, leaf into the moist air
to spin and reweave a lost tribe of yolks
before shocked eyes if the halls were not empty,
the museum-goers not banished
to go sit somewhere on their children
as good parents should. Such is the dream life of hens.

To the doubters who jeer and stare,
call me misguided, I say, there are too many of us
to save; the battle over our souls
was decided long ago anyway,
so why not preach to the bookless chicken?
When they sneer I tell them, if your god is great enough,

lower your nose to an overdue clutch
and thread through the 17,000 pores of each shell
the odor of patience gone sour, sulfurous,
and once it has coursed through your heart,
sat in your stomach,
and you can no longer carry the burden,
return what you have taken to the dirt
which will gladly welcome your offering,
even as you wipe your mouth on your sleeve
and cringe at the chicks sprinting
from the shadow of the car you left parked
under the sign EGGS FOR SALE,
because you are now a part of the ritual,
a necessary antagonist
to a faith no less fragile than your own.

CANSO OF THE DANCING BEARS

They call this place Bulgaria. We still say earth
rising and falling. No matter, we descend
carefully, the three of us, the face of the risen
ground (Musala Peak, if you will), until we get
clear of the fern rot, the fume and hiss of lead
and sulfur mines. Late afternoon, we pass the closed

eyes of a rose farm where night has begun to close
on the empty stomachs of children. The earth
purples one last time and the sun completes its descent.
By morning we reach the caravan, not yet risen
from its slumber. In Greece, where they tend to get
philosophical, even at a circus, the ringmaster leads

the show with our introduction, *The only good bear*—they lead
us quickly in—*is a dancing bear! Keep your eyes closed
and your ears covered if you can't stand to see the earth
shaking bears!* So we dance, or at least we give the sense
of an oafish novice lifting his feet, rising
to the music of a mandolin. How does a bear get

to dance you ask? It starts with a heated needle, we get
a knee to the neck, and then we see a hand leading
us by our pierced muzzles to a pile of ashen coals
where we are taught how mankind once left the earth
when he rose on two feet. Tired of carrying the scent
of our mothers, we rub against the children, then rise

and leave the cow-trodden roads of the country, the ryes
and oats, the beet-laden fields to find work in the ghettos

of Sofia and Varna where we can earn as much as 100 lev
for a wedding, 150 for a birth. In New Delhi, an uncle closed
out his life making 4000 rupees a month. Unearthly
amounts of money can be made if only our descendants

can learn not to hate the children of man. Unruly dissent
will be our undoing if we can not learn how to rise
to the eager crowds, how to make the beautiful get
hysterical with laughter and joy. Don't be misled,
we don't envy man his position, money, or clothes,
nor do we even wish to rid him from the earth.

An unpeopled earth would only beget catastrophe. Chaos
would descend upon us all; the sun would close its eye,
and who would then rise and lead us to the music of our dying?

THE BOX

So I remember the hidden: every night my zaydee
at the ballet watching Zizi
kicking her petite leg above the outstretched claws
of the chorus line as they moved in perfect ruby unison
through third position and then spun
their tulle skirts into a twirl.
All that I know of the interior paramour
I learned from patient zaydee sitting shirtless
off-stage in his old pajamas,
waiting for his crop-haired Zizi to flick
her gypsy fan onto his lap in a mighty crescendo
of leaps and bounds and how could I not love this
and him and all his knowledge of the carnal
life inside the box and so it is
for his sake alone I placate the lovers shaking their fists
in the park, pitched in battle over all the new thinking
outside the box they call their lives
and the faces they make as I pull from my coat
the Lobster Ballet I can never remember
because always I am too busy abandoning their hearts
and engaging the subtle mechanisms of dance
and pointing and blabbering in my delicious nervousness
so that I even forget to tell them they should hum
something Iberian or Basque
and that even "April in Paris" will do
as I gently shake the scarlet dancers of *Carmen*
to stockinged attention and then the watching,
the blessed watching of lovers
rediscovering the pageantry of the interior.

$$\frac{3}{}$$

NORTH FARM

From the hill's crown we can see the weather,
the black-gray bands of thick clouds
gathering like sheep thinned out with a razor.
We're tired and want to sleep, but we're urged

to keep moving. The distant city
is where our guide is taking us. Heat-soaked
afternoon all around us, sparrows cutting
their grooves in and out of the red cedar

canopy we now pass under. Like in a dream
we squint and try to focus our eyes
upon the looming gridlock of leaves.

We are in the dark now. Hand in hand,
we panic and stumble along like shadows
flickering in a sun-forsaken land.

A muddy street, trees hung low with rain,
tamped meadows all around us, we slop into town
and notice the beat-upon gables, the roofs
raked from cornice to eave. Littered all around

us are the badly broken bodies of birds
big and small. On the sill of a window, the silhouette
of a small cat licks its paw, then brushes
its lip, then licks again. In an ice-filled gully crickets

wobble on shaky shoots and work up the momentum
in their legs for a song or two. "Soon you'll eat,"
says our guide, "and be safe." "Draw no attention

to yourself," he says. "Blend in and batten down."
Dusk. Fireflies work hope in their tails.
It had rained before us. It would rain again.

We walk around with our families in tow. The guards advise us
not to ignore the signs: DO NOT FEED THE ANIMALS
and SMOKING PROHIBITED. We see tables
crowded with summer fruit and vegetables.

We watch the hands inspect the recently plucked
for nicks and cuts, bumps and bruises,
that might speak to what goes on below the hardened skin
of the pumpkin, the tender armor of the Brussels.

We all want the answer to the same question:
what does the dark taste like around the peach's knobby heart,
along the zucchini's seeded spine? We all want to sample, to taste

the secret squares of summer corn but no one is willing to pay.
Not my brothers and sisters, not even my mother and father.
No one wants to trade something for something anymore.

To our left are crowded all of the animals who've been chosen
because they are the youngest and therefore the most tender,
or because they are the fattest and can offer the most
to the growling stomachs, the restless tongues.

A goat kicks someone. The guards babble
about their children, their mistresses in the country,
how they like to make them shine their boots
with their coarse midnight hair they will only unbraid

and let fall to their hips before taking to bed. A goat
kicks and is kicked back. Two men, fourteen and sixteen,
run from the thrum-tailed bodies of a honeycomb

they have stoned to the ground because it swayed
like a golden knuckle from a hanging tree
and resembled the sun we had not seen for days.

We gather for breakfast at a table that seats four.
Today we are missing two. Frankie and Johnny
Orowitz never joined us to greet the morning
with prayer and food. Last night, we heard the baying

outside, German shepherds and Dobermans,
and saw the faint flicker of lamps tearing
the dark acres of oak and spruce. Hours later,
in an old tree no more than twelve feet high, joking

guards found them hanging upside down
like corkscrew-necked owls who, although spent,
dreamt they could keep turning. Left in their gowns,

poor Frankie and Johnny now wander in their sleep
down the deserted damp-cold avenues
where the horse-stones are golden and everything is for sale.

In the alley an old grandmother is beaten. My sister tells me
how an old woman, taller and more severe of expression
than the one under siege now, once showed her how to feed
the belly of a fire. Upon arriving, we are taught a lesson:

food is for consumption and not art, science or play.
Yet someone took the risk to show my sister how
to drop food into a fire: one spoonful for protection,
two for health. He strikes her with the heel of his boot now.

A cabbage and milk broth runs into the street's uneven grooves
and already I can see them, hear them even, marching
in their single line, clothed in their red ant regalia, from the guts

of an altar where they have been working. He bludgeons
her and then she learns to eat his whip and for a moment
the cool morning shines once more with all of its old brilliance.

Dressed in gray, a network of angels, they guard night and day
the gates to the city. We say there is no God and laugh;
we say pity the poor angels, lonely, the sick ones who prey
on mites from their bellies before their baths

in the dusty light. They are really not so hard to pity
when you see one weeping after digging a knee in our backs
or biting our hands with rope for the sins of our needy
fathers and mothers. We pity them because they can't

brush their teeth or wear shoes, because they can't escape
their desire to collect our shoestrings and belts, our forks and spoons,
the laundry we bring with us, the unused keys and change

in our pockets, our healthy teeth that will fall out in time.
We pity them the roughshod nest they build out of what we lose
because it will never be finished so long as we are alive.

"DEAD CROSSING, DEAD CROSSING," they shout
this from the sidewalks and the street corners. Black boots
rise and fall in the morning air. Four young men shoulder
the weight of the armless sack our neighbor wears.

He was a few hours away from his next meal, but he got greedy
and stole from the kitchen when no one was looking.
Everyone is always looking. Now he sleeps the sleep
of no dreams and we count him lucky. Lucky

is what we say and then we celebrate, my family and I,
by skinning apples. We take one at a time and quarter
them, tossing seeds and cores to the swine.

They too should feel lucky and celebrate because today
our exhausted masters have made certain
there is room enough for one more of us in the world.

ECLOGUE

Father to Son: The trees are fat with ash
     And horses are dead in the street;
The blast has startled the crows, go shake
     The trunks while I work the peat.

$\dfrac{4}{}$

KARMA

When she came from the East, empty-handed,
the newspapers used words like raiment, blue, shimmers,
to describe her arrival in the hall of immigrants.
Under occupation she scribbled solace.
District offices went empty, the coffee dark and cold,
as we paraded her down the avenues
to the courthouse square where her pink likeness
stood cut in granite. She smiled and waved, bowed
as she left, and we all thought, "Straight to work!"
But she had not come to judge, rather to forget.
When nothing changed, no one noticed. Day to day
we cheered her; meanwhile, she counted the hours
under a birch somewhere, deathless, teaching
the hemorrhaging mouse at her feet about patience.

TWENTY-FIRST CENTURY EXHIBIT

At the Museum of Natural History,
three guards in blue eyed us while the fourth,

shorter than the others, traced our bodies
with a wand. Satisfied, they returned our keys,

coffee, eyeglasses, and marched us into the exhibit
crafted to look like an office purged of its desks,

its loping workers, the maze of gray-board cubicles.
In the center of the room, a water cooler

stood patiently. In vain, we tried to explicate
the intent: "A metaphor for the modern personality,"

said a man with cockroach eyebrows. "No,
it's the perfect marriage of form and content,"

uttered a woman in a beret. Just then, the artist,
who had been hidden among us, crossed the rope

and knelt at the cooler, his lips working the spigot
while the rest of us stared, tongues too dumb

to say anything as the water hiccuped and disappeared.
He gleefully pointed at his rounded belly,

and then waddled to a door without a doorknob
marked with the universal triangle for toilet.

His work begun, he signaled to an unseen hand
to soften the lamps above us to a kinder orange

so he could more easily study us, his creation,
so he could attempt to learn what can't be learned,

like why I hate tuna salad garnished with pickle,
how my father wore it on his sleeve—pink-green

like his heart—the day he busted my nose
for spitting and then again for crying about it.

How could anyone ever know this by looking?
Still, he persisted with the examination

and turned us over in his mind, prizing our flaws
because they conferred character,

even as his own body began to betray him,
the sharp pain in his groin growing sharper.

And if it had been one of us across the rope,
on the rack for art, how long would we have waited

to shout *finito!* or *genius!* once our bladders
had swelled like accordions and we were dancing

our own version of the dervish he was madly spinning?
Bored with ordinary agony, we slouched

toward the tribal wail, the old altar and rot displays
of the twentieth-century wing now under renovation.

IDIOM OF THE HERO

a cento

We are born ruinous: poor mothers cry,
"Was it worth it?" "Was it worth it?"
from wall to wall, like a cradle's rockabye.

Outside on the road, already the appeal of night,
on rusty grass girls receive soldiers
among the blueberry barrens; the soil is tired

And for all this, nature is never spent;
on the wall the dense ivy of executions
always right at hand. Then, under apple trees

in between horror and hunger,
beautiful mythomaniacs with platinum hair,
rebuilding structures, while time, impotent, disintegrates...

My soul is simple; it doesn't think.
Something strange paces there now.
Secrets, yours and mine? Not great secrets.

A time comes when you no longer can say: my God.
You can take my hand, if you pretend
no one conjures our dust.

These things I have—a withered hand—
fœtor, sweat, the stench of stale oranges,
an undisturbed, unbreathing flame,

and tiny sky creatures buried under the snow.
They represent, I fancy, a version of heaven;
We commit them to memory, which is a larger country.

LITTLE ODESSA SOCIAL CLUB

Because my mind is a graveyard
that won't keep its dead I call

for Isaak Babel across the winter air.
If he'd only listen, I'd have him writing

about the Cheka again, food and violence.
When I think about his fate, I always mangle

the details: a steam-filled room,
Stalin's doom, the petite, gloved hand

whistling through the dark at the shaved head
a moon would adore. When night

falls it is always the same: the sun slips
off and all doors lead backstage

where the bereaved are busy begging
for those who have gone before

and before we know it our wish
will be granted when the dead rise

from their tables and Babel calls us
out to the stage where we will fumble

our instruments and mutilate each note
because even the dead need a little something

to lift their feet and dance to.

ON THE LAM

Tonight I sit alone with the wall, staring at its poster
of poached eggs with yellow tights, a piece of bacon
for a hat, announcing the return to prominence
of breakfast when everyone secretly knows
lunch is more deserving. This kind of absurdity
is what keeps me awake at night, tiptoeing
in my socks to re-latch the windows,
to test the locks on the door for the hundredth time
while the couple upstairs sleeps en plein air,
the wind off the harbor thwacking their curtains,
a quilt laid over their bodies like a wing.
She dreams of the fabulous men she has never met,
the ones who will take direction around a body,
who will not drag pleasure home by the hair,
clubbing the red dahlias along the way,
sparing all the others; in her heaven she is chasing
true love, not the man who is cradling her head
in his arm, is now adjusting his hips, is now dreaming
of an Appaloosa from Lascaux.
Tomorrow, she will make the perfect pot of coffee
and walk to the corner where she will meet the man
of her dreams mailing his bills a week early
while the angel from her bed drives into the country
to buy a Bay Mare. Such is life in Utopia.
I am on the run from this murderous peace,
hiding in a basement from the police of Good Intentions
who want to question me about my crooked teeth,
my ugly hands, the mohair jacket I lifted
from someone's chair, its elbows thin, its gilded buttons rotten.
At daybreak I'll carefully slip in among the slacks and skirts

marching to work, but before I go,
before I follow my nose down to the wharf,
before I set sail for better shores
where the children run the docks hawking
scarves and zinnias for the jingle in your pocket,
where their parents still know how to fight and what's better
how to lose themselves in anger, reluctant anger,
the kind we were granted long ago on the eighth day
when He was no longer busy hiding justice in the fang
of each beast, remorse in the shaft of each claw,
and all that lives in my teeth is regret,
sweet regret, pacing its network of black caves
at all hours of the morning, debating the virtues of cobbler
and hunger, the ethics of pity, if one could make a philosophy
out of departures, and before I leave for good
I'll gently turn out my pockets and gather the crumbs
into a pile for the mice in the wall, wipe the filth
from their eyes one last time, perform one more devotion
before I turn my back on this earnest paradise.

A DRESS REHEARSAL FOR THE APOCALYPSE

for Miklós Radnóti

When all the players show up late and no one
can find the accoutrements of elegy,
and even Time saunters his way backstage
while I help History dress like a pilgrim,
despite his protests, and place him left of center—
the side of the road—where he pilfers the poor
saps like myself who believe there is no pity
in death, I must remain faithful
to the customs and decorums of the elegy—
an inborn fear of sex, a holy reverence
for the cordless communiqué; so delicate
History I prop with baskets of toes and teeth,
nipple and tongue, and have I mentioned song
has always been my curse and I wonder what
will Death the critic write about the chorus
in the morning's edition and how hard it is
to find a romantic nickelodeon these days
because they are all obsessed with dying
and who knew that when we rehearsed our lines
about his love of potatoes, cleaned and shaven,
pocketfuls dancing in the arms of a black pot
we would all agree this sounded trite, yet, if not
through food how else convince an audience
of the imminent resurrection in Act Four?
History howls for direction so I take him
by the sleeve and remind him how the hero
was lost to nineteen forty-four, to the black dirt
of Hungary and then how like Lazarus
he rose from the darkest beds in Abda

after six years, dirty-eared and unshaven,
and brought a message we could not abide
because he was still only a man in a man's shape.

BLOODHOUNDS

Once they had been replaced by people
with noses equally capable of navigating
a complex sea of collapsed rebar and concrete
to a single, drifting mote of skin,
they sought other employment. The truth
was clear: we didn't need walking,
shamefully at times, to a dry median
during rush hour, nor training to say *Here,*
dig here, this one can make it. Out of work,
some hung up their fedoras, put away
the spy glass and went to the country to herd,
but discovered sheep stink, goats too,
and that horses can't be trusted.
In the city, others tried guarding banks
but were too often lulled to sleep
by the dull odor of husbands and wives.
Soon the newspapers began to cry
what dogs could already hear: "mongrels,"
"lazy," "Take our jobs, is what they do."
Slowly, many drifted back to the swamps
of long rifles, of coons piled on a porch
ahum with the nineteenth century. Years later,
when hardly anyone remembered them,
a lone pack did what celebrities do when they fall
from favor, they answered the call of Hollywood
to join the cameras and props on the set
of the new *Singing School.* That first night
we watched them warm up by howling
the vowels: over and over the long O
drew from the black and tan chorus a wail

from the Old World, a helpless moan
that broke the backs of centuries
each time it passed through the sad, bent halo
of their mouths. They were a hit
because karaoke was fashionable again,
as was suffering, as was pity,
and so the episodes kept coming, cabled
week after week into the dark living rooms
where our beautiful, intelligent race sat
in the raw hours, attentive, sniffing the air,
waiting for a sign in those throaty baritones
that we might yet find another life.

NOTES

PAGE 12

"Presidential Portrait" is a response to Jonathan Yeo's collage "Bush 2007."

PAGE 30

"Winter" owes a debt to Flemish painter Abel Grimmer's "L'Hiver."

PAGE 55

"Idiom of the Hero" borrows its title from Wallace Stevens, and each line from the following sources:

1. John Donne: "An Anatomy of the World," line 95.
2. Miklós Radnóti: "The Terrifying Angel," transl. by Stephen Berg.
3. Joseph Brodsky: "Lullaby of Cape Cod," XI, transl. by Anthony Hecht.
4. Yannis Ritsos: "Dusk," transl. by Paul Merchant.
5. Zbigniew Herbert: "Naked Town," transl. by Czesław Miłosz and Peter Dale Scott.
6. Amy Clampitt: "Midsummer in the Blueberry Barrens."
7. Gerard Manley Hopkins: "God's Grandeur."
8. Zbigniew Herbert: "A Halt," transl. by Miłosz and Scott.
9. Czesław Miłosz: "To Robinson Jeffers," transl. by Miłosz and Richard Lourie.
10. Miroslav Holub: "Suffering," transl. by Ian Milner and George Theiner.
11. Adam Wazyk: "Sketch for a Memoir," transl. by Miłosz.
12. Aleksander Wat: "Songs of a Wanderer," II, Miłosz.
13. Fernandoa Pessoa: "If they want me to be a mystic, fine. So I'm a mystic," transl. by Edwin Honig.
14. Osip Mandelstam: "Let me be in your service," transl. by W.S. Merwin and Clarence Brown.
15. Czesław Miłosz: "Elegy for N.N.," transl. by Miłosz and Lawrence Davis.
16. Carlos Drummond de Andrade: "Your Shoulders Hold up the World," transl. by Mark Strand.
17. Eugenio Montale: "Indian Serenade," transl. by Jonathan Galassi.
18. Paul Celan: "Psalm," transl. by Michael Hamburger.
19. Hart Crane: "The Moth That God Made Blind."

20. Ezra Pound: "Canto xiv."
21. Elizabeth Bishop: "Over 2,000 Illustrations and a Complete Concordance."
22. Federico García Lorca: "Blind Panorama of New York," transl. by Greg Simon and Steven F. White.
23. James Merrill: "Willoware Cup."
24. Joseph Brodsky: "Variation in V."

PAGE 61

"Bloodhounds" is indebted to "The Body-Sniffers" by Sharon Olds.

ACKNOWLEDGMENTS

My thanks to the editors of the following publications in which these poems first appeared.

Alimentum: "While Waiting for the Resurrection"

American Poetry Review, "Our Prophets"

Blackbird: "The Life of the Party"

Boulevard: "Castrato," "The Home Front," "Laika," "Bloodhounds"

Cortland Review: "Egg Ministry"

High Chair: "North Farm"

Literary Imagination: "Winter"

Margie: "Canso of the Dancing Bears"

New Orleans Review: "Eclogue"

Oranges & Sardines: "Karma"

Ploughshares: "Dumb Luck"

Poetry International: "On the Lam"

Slate: "The Box," "Twenty-first Century Exhibit"

Threepenny Review: "Presidential Portrait"

"British Birds in Manhattan," "Little Odessa Social Club," "Idiom of the Hero," "A Dress Rehearsal for the Apocalypse," "A Model for the Priesthood," and "The Family Artist" originally appeared in *Narrative* magazine.

"Laika" and "Bloodhounds" were part of a group of poems selected as the winner of the 2010 *Boulevard* Emerging Poets contest.

"A Model for the Priesthood" was awarded third place in *Narrative* magazine's First Annual Poetry Contest.

Endless gratitude to *The American Poetry Review*, Copper Canyon Press, the Honickman Foundation, and Elizabeth Scanlon for her wisdom, guidance, and most of all, her limitless patience. I am grateful to Valerie Brewster for enduring my countless requests with grace as she brought this book to life.

Much appreciation to the Bread Loaf Writers' Conference, the Provincetown Fine Arts Work Center, Idyllwild Arts, and the New York State Summer Writer's Institute for their support and for welcoming me into their communities. Many thanks to all my teachers, in particular Miles Wilson, Kathleen Peirce and Cyrus Cassells. For the gift of family and community, a huge hug to my Voltron brothers and sisters Marie Mockett, Dolen Perkins-Valdez, Heidi Durrow, James Arthur, Elena Passarello, Kara Candito, Celeste Ng, and especially those who bravely suffered this book in earlier versions, Eduardo C. Corral, Al Heathcock, Jim Ruland, Sasha West, Dave Lucas, and Hasanthika Sirisena. To David Turkle, endless gratitude. Many thanks to Erin Evans and Maggie Blake for their faith and for letting the circle be unbroken. I owe a special debt of gratitude to everyone who helped shepherd this book in one way or another, in particular C. Dale Young, Robert Pinsky, Alan Shapiro, Leslie Harrison, Jon Marc Smith, and Peter Campion.

My deepest gratitude to Tom Sleigh for his encouragement and support of this collection.

To Philip Levine for his heart, honesty, friendship, and the example of his life in poetry, thank you for helping me find the path.

Most importantly, I would like to thank D'Andra for all the love, sacrifice, and unwavering belief in the face of all my doubts that the impossible would one day happen. You are the sun that rises and sets above my country.

This book is set in Adobe Caslon, designed by Carol Twombly, with titles set in ITC Founders' Caslon Twelve, designed by Justin Howes. Both faces are based on type cut by William Caslon in the early 1700s. Caslon types continued to be popular, especially in America where Caslon was used to print the Declaration of Independence. Both Twombly and Howes worked from original Caslon specimens. Where Adobe Caslon is a revival for contemporary expectations and technology, Founders' Caslon retains the organic texture of the original letter-press printing.

CPSIA information can be obtained at www.ICGtesting.com
Printed in the USA
BVOW04s1902161014

371148BV00002B/15/P